Football

SPORTS SKILLS

Clive Gifford

W

FRANKLIN WATTS
LONDON • SYDNEY

Franklin Watts
Published in Great Britain in 2017 by
The Watts Publishing Group

Credits

Series Editor: Adrian Cole
Art direction: Peter Scoulding
Series designed and created for
 Franklin Watts by Storeybooks
Designer: Rita Storey
Editor: Nicola Barber
Photography: Tudor Photography,
 Banbury (unless otherwise stated)

Dewey number 796.3'34
ISBN 978 1 4451 4094 0

Printed in China

MIX
Paper from
responsible sources
FSC
www.fsc.org
FSC® C104740

Franklin Watts
An imprint of Hachette Children's Group
Part of The Watts Publishing Group
Carmelite House
50 Victoria Embankment
London EC4Y 0DZ

An Hachette UK Company
www.hachette.co.uk

www.franklinwatts.co.uk

Note: At the time of going to press, the
statistics and player profiles in this book were
up to date. However, due to some players'
active participation in the sport, it is possible
that some of these may now be out of date.

Picture credits

Action Plus p9b; p11t; p13b; p20;
Shutterstock/ Kostas Koutsaftikis p8;
Shutterstock/ Christian Bertrand p9t; p13b;
Shutterstock/Maxisport p14t; p20; p25t;
Shutterstock/ Laszlo Szirtesi p25b; Shutterstock/
Marcos Mesa Sam Wordley p26

Cover images: Tudor Photography, Banbury.

All photos posed by models.

Thanks to Matthew Carberry, Mark Fenemore,
Henry Glendinning, Yannick Nkwanyvo, and
Carl Taylor..

The Publisher would like to thank Banbury
School for use of the football pitch.

Previously published by Franklin Watts as
Know Your Sport: Football

Taking part in sport is a fun
way to get fit, but like any
form of physical exercise it has
an element of risk, particularly
if you are unfit, overweight
or suffer from any medical
conditions. It is advisable
to consult a healthcare
professional before beginning
any programme of exercise.

Contents

Introduction

Football is the world's most popular sport. Hundreds of millions of people across the globe either watch or play this all-action game. No single individual invented the sport. Games played with a ball and feet have existed all over the world for hundreds of years, but football, as we know it, began in the 19th century.

Aim of the Game

A football match lasts 90 minutes, divided into two 45-minute halves. There are 11 players on each team, some of whom can be replaced during a match by substitutes.

Players can use any parts of their bodies to move the ball – except their arms and their hands. (The exception is the goalkeeper – see pages 26–27.) The aim of the game is to score goals. A goal is awarded by the referee – the official who runs the game – when the ball completely crosses the goal-line between the two goalposts. The team with more goals at the end of the game wins.

The Pitch

• A full-sized football pitch is a rectangle between 90m and 120m long, and 45m to 90m wide.

• Its long edges are the sidelines, and the shorter edges at each end are goal-lines.

• A halfway line divides the pitch in two. In the middle of this line is the centre spot, where the ball is placed before a match begins.

Strikers are the players who usually score goals while the backs mainly defend, making sure opponents do not score goals. Players in the midfield can play either defence or attack, depending on the rest of the team.

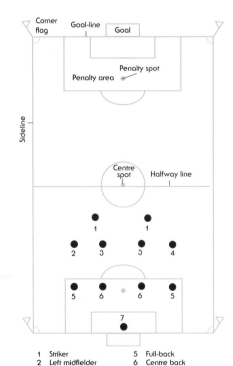

1 Striker	5	Full-back
2 Left midfielder	6	Centre back
3 Central midfielder	7	Goalkeeper
4 Right midfielder		

Restarting the Game

When the whole of the ball crosses the sideline or goal-line and leaves the pitch, the game stops. Play can be restarted in a number of ways depending on where the ball went out and which side touched it last. For example, if the ball crosses the goal-line (outside the goal) and the attacking team touched it last, a goal-kick is awarded to the defending team.

Football for All

The beauty of football is that it is a simple sport that needs little equipment. Informal games can be held in parks with fewer than 11 players on each team. One of the most popular smaller versions is five-a-side, often played indoors in sports halls. Five-a-side matches are great for building up skills and fitness to play the full game.

Taking a Throw-in

If the ball completely crosses a sideline, a throw-in is awarded to the team who did not touch the ball last. To perform a throw-in, the player must keep his feet on the ground and behind the sideline. Both hands must be kept on the ball as he brings it back over his head and then forward to release it into play.

Taking a Corner

If the ball crosses the goal-line (outside the goal) and the defending team touched it last, then a corner is awarded. The ball is placed in the corner quadrant and the attacking player attempts to pass short to a team-mate, or cross it towards the goal to create an attack.

The Game

Football matches are run according to the laws of the game. The referee is the person who controls the game with the help of two assistants who run along the sidelines, and a fourth official who helps the referee.

The Referee's Duties

The referee makes sure a match is played within the laws of the game. It is up to the referee to decide if a goal has been scored or whether to award a free-kick or penalty. The referee's decision is always final. The referee is also responsible for timekeeping.

Foul!

Fouls include tripping, kicking, pushing and pulling on a shirt to hold back an opponent. The referee punishes a foul by awarding a free-kick to the other team. If the foul takes place inside the penalty area, the punishment is usually a penalty kick at goal.

Red and Yellow Cards

Apart from a whistle, the referee has two other important pieces of equipment: a yellow and a red card. If a bad foul is committed, the referee can 'book' or 'caution' the player responsible by raising the yellow card. An even more serious foul can result in a red card, which means a player is sent off. The player has to leave the pitch and the team continues one player down for the rest of the game. A player who receives two yellow cards during the course of a match is automatically sent off.

Wayne Rooney of Manchester United looks up before passing the ball in a UEFA match against Greek team Olympiacos in 2014.

This player is being shown a yellow card by the referee (see above).

Free-kicks

There are two types of free-kick:

• A direct free-kick can be struck straight at goal.

• An indirect free-kick has to be touched by another player first.

On the Spot

A penalty kick is taken from the penalty spot, a little under 12m from the goal-line. Only the penalty-taker and the goalkeeper are allowed in the penalty area until the ball has been kicked. A penalty is an excellent chance for a team to score. Penalty-takers aim to place the ball in the corner of the net or to beat the goalkeeper with a powerful shot. Goalkeepers try to guess the direction of the ball in advance in order to make a save.

Shoot-outs

A penalty shoot-out is used to decide the result of a game that has ended in a draw. Teams take alternate penalties to determine the winner. If after each side has taken five penalties, the scores are even, penalties go into dramatic 'sudden death'. Shoot-outs have been used to decide many quarter- and semi-finals and even the finals of World Cups – the men's 1994 and 2006 World Cups, and the women's 1999 and 2011 World Cups all finished with penalty shoot-outs.

Action from the Women's Football Spanish League in a match between Barcelona and Real Zaragoza. Barcelona have come top of the Spanish women's premier division in 2012, 2013 and 2014.

The Biggest Competition of All

The FIFA World Cup is the biggest and most prestigious football competition in the world. First staged in 1930 in Uruguay, it is held every four years between the world's best national teams. Brazil has won the competition five times, more than any other side. The women's World Cup began in 1991 and has become a highly popular competition, with teams such as Germany, USA, Norway, Japan and Sweden at the forefront.

Training to Play

Playing football at a high level requires years of training. Even the world's greatest players have to continue to work hard at their skills and fitness. Young players hoping to match their heroes must be prepared to practise whenever they can.

Fit for the Job

Professional footballers spend much of their time between matches training to build their speed, strength and stamina – the ability to work at peak performance for long periods. As a junior footballer, you should not worry about strength and gym training, but you should try to get as fit as possible by running, taking part in other sports and playing lots of practice matches, as well as performing drills in training or with friends.

Getting Warmer

Before playing a match or training, always warm up and stretch beforehand. This helps to loosen your muscles and prepare your body for the physical challenge ahead. Warming up involves:

- running on the spot
- jogging round the pitch
- star jumps
- stretches, including back, side, groin and upper and lower leg-muscle stretches performed under the eye of your coach.

Stretches

Players perform a series of stretches to the key muscles in their legs, arms and back before starting a game. These stretches help them perform at their best and to prevent injuries.

Kitted Up

In matches, a football team (with the exception of the goalkeeper) must all wear the same colour strip, consisting of shirts, shorts and socks. Socks are kept up with elastic or tape. Inside the socks, good shin pads, which protect the bony front of your lower leg, should be worn. In training and practice matches, wear comfortable clothing that is not too tight. A tracksuit is very useful to keep you warm before and after games or training. Do not forget a water bottle to take regular sips from in training.

A Good Fit

Good football boots are essential. Do not be concerned whether they are endorsed by a star player – what matters is that the boot fits your foot well. A good boot should be flexible, but support your ankle well and be made from soft leather that allows your foot to feel the ball. Boots come with plastic studs moulded into the sole, or with screw-in studs. Check with your coach that your studs are the right length for the pitch and that they are all screwed in firmly.

Mia Hamm

United States of America
Date of birth: 17 March, 1972
Position: Striker
Height: 1.65m
International caps: 275
International goals: 158

Through training hard and practising, Mia Hamm became the youngest-ever US Women's team player when she made her debut at the age of 15. She proved a lethal goalscorer and held the record for international goals until fellow American, Abby Wambach, overtook her. Part of the gifted US women's team that won both the 1991 and 1999 World Cups, Hamm also won two Olympic gold medals for football. She is one of only two female players to appear in the FIFA 100, a list of the 125 greatest living players chosen by footballing legend Pelé to mark the centenary of FIFA IN 2004.

These footballers are doing a 'pass and move' exercise in a small area marked with cones. They are practising making short, accurate passes then moving quickly into space in time to receive a return pass.

KK484714

Ball Control

You can be the greatest passer or shooter in the world, but unless you can control the ball well, you will not have much chance to show your skills. Work on your ball-control skills before and during training and matches.

First Touch

A ball often comes towards you at high speed. Sometimes, it can be knocked onwards by giving it a light touch, or glance, off your head or foot. Many times, though, you need to bring the ball under control so that it is at your feet, allowing you to pass, cross or shoot. A ball that comes towards you gently across the pitch can be stopped by putting your foot on the top of the ball. This is called trapping.

Cushioning not Pushing

Cushioning is a way of slowing the ball down. You need to keep your body relaxed so that the ball does not fly or bounce off. As the ball makes contact with a part of your body, you bring that part of your body back and down to cushion the ball's impact.

Sidefoot Cushion

1 The inside part of your boot can be used to cushion the ball. Here, the player has turned his foot outwards, presenting the inside of his boot to the ball.

2 Keeping his balance, the player brings his foot back and down as the ball makes impact.

3 The ball drops to the floor allowing him to move it away with the outside of his foot.

Thigh Cushion

1 The player lifts his leg so that his thigh is almost parallel to the ground. Using his arms for balance, he watches the ball as it comes in.

2 The player pulls his leg back and down as the ball makes impact. The ball should fall gently so that he can use his feet to get it under control.

Body Works

Unless you are a goalkeeper, touching the ball deliberately with your hands or arms will result in the referee blowing the whistle for handball and giving a free-kick or penalty to the other side. When the ball falls from a high position, you must use your chest or your thigh to bring the ball under control.

What Next?

Once the ball is under control at your feet, you have several options. First, look up and be aware of what is happening on the pitch.

• If a team-mate is free and in a good position, you can make a quick pass.

• If there is plenty of space ahead you can run with the ball or, if you are close to the goal, you can strike a shot.

• If an opponent is closing in on you, look to make a clearance upfield or a quick pass (lay-off).

• If you are under pressure in a defensive position and in danger of losing the ball, put the ball out of play for a throw-in or corner to the other team.

Whilst playing for AC Milan, the Brazilian midfielder, Kaká, performs a chest cushion. He leans back as the ball arrives to kill its speed. The ball will drop to the floor in front of him for his feet to control.

Passing

When one team has the ball under control, the ball is said to be in the team's possession. Once in possession, the players can move the ball around the pitch by passing it to each other. Good, accurate passing allows a team to stay in possession as it builds an attack.

Pass Types

The most common pass is the side-foot pass. It works well for distances up to about 20m. It can also be used for close, accurate shots on goal. The more powerful instep drive (see page 15) is used for longer passes and shots.

Ronaldo

Portugal
Date of birth: 5 February, 1985
Position: Forward
Height: 1.85m
International caps: 135
International goals: 66

Ranked as one of the best players in the world, Cristiano Ronaldo played for Manchester United from 2003 to 2009. He was named FIFA World Player of the Year in 2008. In 2009, he became the world's most expensive player when he moved to Real Madrid in a transfer worth £80 million (however, since 2013 that record has been overtaken – see page 28). He first played for the Portuguese national team in 2003, and has since been capped over 100 times. He is Portugal's top international goalscorer of all time, and became captain of the national team in 2008.

Side-foot Pass

1 The player places his standing (right) foot beside the ball. He turns his passing foot outwards so that the inside of his boot will make contact with the ball. The passing foot is parallel to the ground.

2 With his body over the ball, the player swings his foot, stroking through the middle of the ball. The passing foot follows through and points to the target of the pass.

Instep Drive

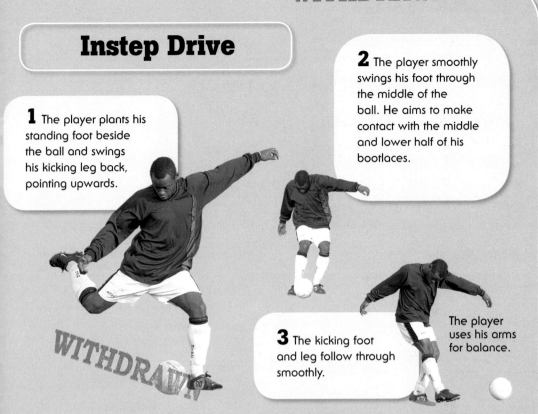

1 The player plants his standing foot beside the ball and swings his kicking leg back, pointing upwards.

2 The player smoothly swings his foot through the middle of the ball. He aims to make contact with the middle and lower half of his bootlaces.

3 The kicking foot and leg follow through smoothly.

The player uses his arms for balance.

The Right Strength

Players can vary the speed and distance of a pass by swinging their leg back more or less, and bringing their kicking foot down faster or slower through the ball. Judging how much force is needed to make a pass is vital. It comes only with a lot of practice.

Adding Height

Sometimes it is necessary to hit the ball a bit higher in the air, particularly for defensive clearances and crosses when the ball is put into the penalty area for an attacker to head or shoot. With the instep drive, the player can get extra height on the ball by leaning back a little and hitting through the lower half of the ball.

Practice Makes Perfect

It is important to practise your passing as often as possible. Passing in triangles with two team-mates, as the three of you jog and sprint around the pitch, is a good way to practise passing to team-mates while they are on the move.

Feet First

Coaches are extremely keen on players working on their passing with their weaker foot. This is because a player who can play and pass equally well with both their right and left feet is a real asset to any team.

On the Ball

When players receive the ball, they need to be aware of what is happening on the pitch. They must watch out for approaching opponents and spot where their team-mates are. Keeping control of the ball, turning and running with it are all essential skills.

Shielding

Shielding the ball is a way of preventing an opponent from getting to the ball. A player puts their body between the ball and the opponent, to try to keep possession.

Turning

When in space, a player can turn with the ball simply by rolling it to one side with the sole of their boot and swivelling their body to move in another direction. When space is tight, they can use a skill called a hook turn. The player leans in the direction that they wish to turn. They hook their boot around the ball and as their body turns, they drag or flick the ball in the same direction with their foot.

Shielding

1 To shield the ball, the player positions his body between the ball and the player from the other team. The shielding player must not back into or push his opponent, but he can keep his arms out for balance.

2 The player is aware of where his opponent is and keeps moving to keep his body between the opponent and the ball. He must keep the ball under control and make his next move, such as a pass back. If his opponent comes round the side, he may be able to turn the other way and sprint clear.

Running with the Ball

When players receive the ball, they will often look to run with the ball into space ahead of them. They keep their head up as much as possible to watch how the game is developing in front of them. The key skill is to maintain their speed by pushing the ball far enough ahead of them to allow them to run well, but not so far that they lose control of the ball.

Dribbling

Dribbling, is running with the ball, but with the player keeping it under close control with a series of small taps and nudges. Dribbling can be fun and looks exciting, but it is a risky move as an opponent may win the ball with a tackle. Dribbling is best done when attacking and in the other side's half of the pitch.

Dummying

Good dribbling often requires a lot of speed or trickery. Players may twist and turn while dribbling and may also use dummies to trick opponents. A simple dummy is to drop one shoulder and lean in one direction. This may make the opponent think you are heading one way, only for you to twist and move away in another direction.

Dummying

1 The player on the ball drops his right shoulder and appears to be heading to his left. The defender starts to lean that way to cover his opponent's run.

2 The attacker pushes off his left foot sharply to head to his right. The defender has been wrong-footed and is off balance. The attacker can run past.

Attacking

A moment of individual brilliance or skill in attack can sometimes create a good chance to score a goal. However, most goals come from players working hard as a team to build attacks.

Space and Pace

As an attack develops, attackers look for areas of space into which they can run to receive the ball. Frequently, an attacker is marked closely by a defender. They try to get free of their marker by pretending to move in one direction, only to cut away and sprint hard in a different direction.

Working Together

Attackers can work together to create a good goalscoring chance. One method is called an overlap. This is where an attacker runs down the side of the pitch to receive the ball. This player may then be able to continue and cross the ball into the penalty area. Another method of attack is to make a run that is followed by players from the other side. This can draw defenders away from an area of the pitch, leaving space for another attacker to run into.

Cutting Away from a Marker

The attacker (in blue) spots his team-mate on the ball and looks to get away from his marker (in white).

He starts to cut away sharply from his marker at the same time as his team-mate hits a pass. He keeps his eye on the ball hoping to collect the pass.

One-Two Pass

One-Two Pass

The one-two or wall pass is a key way of getting past a defender and furthering an attack. A player passes to a team-mate and as soon as they make the pass, they sprint past the defender.

1 The first attacker passes to his team-mate and sprints hard past the defender.

The receiver may control the ball rapidly or may hit the ball first time. The aim is to pass the ball behind the defender and into space for the first attacker to run on to and control. One-two passes are frequently made using side-foot passes.

2 The second attacker receives the ball and makes a quick, accurate pass behind the defender.

3 The first attacker runs on to the ball. He is clear of the defender who has been cut out by the two passes.

Goalscoring

Goalscoring requires an eye for a goal chance and the skill to take that chance with a shot or header. Goals can be spectacular long-range shots or simple tap-ins. Being in the right position at the right time is crucial.

A Cool Head

Players who score regularly manage to keep their cool when a chance arrives. They have to weigh up the situation very quickly and decide where to aim and what sort of shot to use. In many attacks, a chance to hit a shot disappears as quickly as it occurs. A player has to decide to shoot rapidly or pass to a team-mate in a better position.

Hot Shots

A shot needs the right mixture of power and accuracy. Sometimes, a shot can be steered into a corner from close range with a side-foot pass. At other times, a more powerful shot is required. Top strikers try to aim for the part of the goal the goalkeeper is furthest away from, or least expects the ball to go. If unsure, you should aim for the corners of the goal.

Pelé

Brazil
Date of birth: 23 October, 1940
Position: Striker
Height: 1.78m
International caps: 92
International goals: 77

Pelé is probably the greatest footballer who ever lived. A strong, skilful attacker, he possessed great awareness of others on the pitch. He scored over 1,000 goals for one Brazilian club, Santos, and remains the youngest goalscorer at the World Cup finals (age 17). Pelé won three World Cups with Brazil (1958, 1962 and 1970). When he retired from Santos in 1974, the club also retired his famous number 10 shirt.

Goal of the Year

A stunning goal scored by Irish footballer Stephanie Roche for Peamount United against Wexford Youths was runner-up in FIFA's Goal of the Year award in 2014. The goals that came first and third were both scored in the 2014 World Cup.

On Target

Junior players sometimes find that many of their shots sail high or wide of the target. Practice is the key to good shooting, as well as remembering a number of key points:

- Hit through the middle of the ball not the side or the bottom of it.
- Plant your standing foot beside the ball with your toes pointing to the target.
- Avoid leaning back or stretching for the shot.
- Keep your eyes on the ball throughout the shot.

Heading for Goal

Heading is used in many situations in a match, from clearing the ball out of defence (see page 23) to making a pass to a team-mate. When aiming to score a goal with a header, players try hard to get over the ball and keep their header down.

Goals from Set Plays

Free-kicks from around the penalty area offer a good chance for a shot at goal, but the defensive team will often try to block the shot by arranging players into a defensive wall. One way of beating the wall is to pass the ball to the side so that another attacker can have a clear shot at goal. Another way is to bend the ball around the wall using an outside or inside swerve shot. Swerves are very tricky skills to learn. To bend the ball with the outside of your right foot, for example, kick through the left side of the ball with the outside of the boot. Your kicking foot should follow through across your body and the ball should fly away, heading first to the left before bending to the right during its flight.

Heading Down

1 The player bends his body and neck back a little and pushes his head forward to meet the ball. He times his jump so that he is at the top of it as he meets the ball. He keeps his eyes open and watches the ball as it travels towards him.

2 Slightly above the ball, he pushes through the ball with the middle of his forehead. He tries to keep his neck muscles firm to direct the ball forwards and down towards the goal.

Defending

When team-mates lose possession of the ball they have to start defending. Players must work together as a team to stop their opponents from scoring, and to try to win the ball back.

Defenders

Most teams play with four defenders (see page 6), two centre backs in the middle of the defence and two full-backs, one for each side of the pitch. The centre backs have to be very good at heading the ball so that they can deal with crosses into the penalty area. Full-backs have to patrol their side of the pitch and be good at jockeying (see below) and tackling as well as being able to pass or carry the ball forwards to start an attack.

Teamwork and Marking

Defending is not just for the defenders. The whole side must work together to defend. Team-mates get themselves between the attack and their goal and may man-mark opponents. This means staying relatively close to an opponent to make it hard for them to receive the ball, and staying between them and the goal to make it hard for them to score.

Jockeying

When you are the nearest defender to an opponent with the ball, try to close them down (get a metre or so away from them) and delay their progress. This technique is called jockeying and it can often pressure the attacker into making a mistake.

Jockeying

1 The defender closest to the opponent keeps his eye on the ball as he jockeys his opponent. He stays balanced and ready to move in any direction.

2 A second defender moves in to support his team-mate.

Jockeying an opponent can give your team-mates time to get themselves into good defensive positions and to support you.

Clearing the Ball

Kicks or headers can be used to clear the ball away from your own goal and out of danger. If you find yourself under pressure, consider putting the ball out for a throw-in or hitting it long up the pitch. When you have time on the ball, aim to pass to one of your team-mates who is in space.

Defensive Header

The defender makes a defensive clearing header, using his forehead slightly tilted back to send the ball up and away from his side's penalty area.

Top Tips for Defenders

• **Communicate** – if you want the keeper to receive a back-pass you have to tell them.

• **Listen** – to your team-mates. They can steer you in the right direction.

• **Have patience** – keep trying and attackers will eventually make mistakes.

• **Watch** – keep your eye on the ball at all times.

• **Be prepared** – bend your knees, stay on your toes and be prepared to move sideways or backwards at speed.

Tackling

The aim of tackling is to remove the ball from another player's possession. Ideally, by tackling your opponent you will gain possession of the ball. All players, not just defenders, need to know how to make good, clean tackles that will win the ball without fouling the opponent.

Block Tackle

The most commonly used tackle is called the block tackle. It can be used from the front or from the side and, done well, will enable you to come away with the ball under your control.

Quick Thinking

Sometimes, quick thinking can be enough to win the ball without tackling. For example, an opponent may control the ball poorly or push it too far ahead of their feet. A quick-thinking defender may be able to nip in and get to the ball first.

Interception

Good players stay alert for the chance of a weak pass or one that is not on target. They may be able to charge in and make an interception – taking the ball away before it reaches an opponent.

Front Block Tackle

1 In the front block tackle, the tackler (right) moves close to the opponent and gets his body weight over the foot with which he is going to make the tackle. Using the inside of his foot, and with the foot level with the pitch, the tackler strikes the centre of the ball firmly. This removes the ball from the opponent's control.

2 Having released the ball, the tackler (in blue) seeks to get the ball under control and moves away from his opponent.

Poke Tackle

A poke tackle is when the ball is stabbed away from an opponent, usually with the toe or instep of the boot nearest the ball. It can be useful to remove the ball from an attacker's control, but does not guarantee that the ball ends up under your control. Poke tackles are often used to stop a winger heading down the sideline, by pushing the ball out for a throw-in.

Falling Foul

Tackles have to be very well timed, otherwise there is the danger of giving away a foul (see page 8). This can lead to a free-kick close to your goal or, worse, a penalty. Aim to make contact with the ball first, not the player, and do not kick, shove or pull your opponent. Whenever possible, try to make a tackle that leaves you standing on your feet, ready for the next piece of action.

Thiago Silva

Brazil
Date of birth: 22 September, 1984
Position: Centre back
Height: 1.83m
International caps: 59
International goals: 4

Thiago Silva has been described as 'one of Brazil's best-ever defenders' and as 'one of the best defenders in the world'. He is a tactical player with great positional sense. He is also fast, strong and good in the air.

In his early career he overcame tuberculosis (TB) which stopped him playing for a year. He almost gave up but was persuaded to try again and came back in 2006. Just two years later AC Milan payed £9 million to sign him. Since then he has captained the Brazil team and also his new club, Paris Saint-Germain, who paid Milan £37 million to to add him to their team.

János Szabó of Paks makes a sliding tackle against Somalia from Ferencváros. In a sliding tackle, the defender slides across the ground to hook the ball away from the opponent's feet. Sliding tackles should only be used when other, safer types of tackle cannot be performed.

Goalkeeping

A goalkeeper's job is like no other footballer's. They must organise their team's defence and use great skill, awareness – and sometimes bravery – to stop goals.

Back-pass Rule

The goalkeeper is the only player allowed to handle the ball – but only inside their own penalty area. The goalkeeper is not allowed to handle the ball when a team-mate passes the ball back using a foot or leg. Then the keeper must kick, head or chest the ball clear. This is known as the back-pass rule.

Ball-handling

Keepers need to stay alert at all times and on the balls of their feet when facing an attack. Whenever possible, they try to get their body behind the ball to act as a barrier. They spread their fingers around the back and sides of the ball, and gather it into the body to protect it.

When they have to make a diving save, keepers take a step towards the side of the goal to which the ball is heading and spring off the foot nearest the ball. Catching the ball or using the palm of the hand to push it round the post, keepers try to land on their side with their body relaxed as they hit the ground.

Punch or Palm

Sometimes, a keeper cannot be sure they can catch the ball. In these cases, they have two options.

- They can punch the ball firmly away from the danger area. Keepers try to use both hands to clear the ball a long distance.
- They may also use their hands to push or palm the ball around the post or crossbar.

Iker Casillas is at full stretch as he makes a spectacular save during the UEFA Champions League in 2013. The Spanish player is considered to be one of the greatest goalkeepers of all time.

Ball in Play

Once the ball in is a keeper's hands, they have six seconds to release it back into play. Goalkeepers have a choice of throwing or kicking the ball to one of their team-mates. A quick, accurate pass or throw can help start an attack.

Taking a High Ball

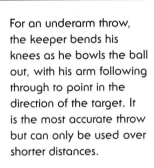

For an underarm throw, the keeper bends his knees as he bowls the ball out, with his arm following through to point in the direction of the target. It is the most accurate throw but can only be used over shorter distances.

1 A high ball, such as a cross, can be caught by a keeper. The keeper turns his body to face the ball and times his jump off one foot, stretching his arms up and outwards.

2 The keeper aims to meet the ball at its highest point and tries to catch it in front of his head if possible. Once safely caught, he bends his elbows to bring the ball into his body.

3 As he falls, the keeper gathers the ball safely into his body.

Statistics and Records

FIFA World Cup

Date	Winners	Runners-up
1930	Uruguay	Argentina
1934	Italy	Czechoslovakia
1938	Italy	Hungary
1950	Uruguay	Brazil
1954	W Germany	Hungary
1958	Brazil	Sweden
1962	Brazil	Czechoslovakia
1966	England	W Germany
1970	Brazil	Italy
1974	W Germany	Netherlands
1978	Argentina	Netherlands
1982	Italy	W Germany
1986	Argentina	W Germany
1990	W Germany	Argentina
1994	Brazil	Italy
1998	France	Brazil
2002	Brazil	Germany
2006	Italy	France
2010	Spain	Netherlands
2014	Germany	Argentina

FIFA Women's World Cup

Date	Winners	Runners-up
1991	USA	Norway
1995	Norway	Germany
1999	USA	China
2003	Germany	Sweden
2007	Germany	Brazil
2011	Japan	USA
2015	USA	Japan

Most Goals in International Football

Women	Abby Wambach (USA)	184
Men	Ali Daei (Iran)	109

Longest Clean Sheet (no goal let in) in International Football

1,142 minutes   Dino Zoff (Italy)

Most Goals Scored in a World Cup Match (Team)

12 goals   Austria 7 – Switzerland 5
1954 World Cup

Top Goalscorer in one World Cup Tournament

13 goals   Just Fontaine (France)   1958

Top Goalscorer in the World Cup

16 goals Miroslav Klose (Germany)
2002, 2006, 2010, 2014

World Record Transfer Fee

£89 million   Paul Pogba from Juventus to Manchester United in 2016

Most International Caps

Women:	352 Kristine Lilly (USA)
Men:	184 Ahmed Assan (Egypt)
England:	125 Peter Shilton
	150 Fara Williams
Scotland:	102 Kenny Dalglish
	193 Gemma Fay
Wales:	92 Neville Southall
	92 Michelle Green
N Ireland:	119 Pat Jennings
	125 Emma Byrne

Glossary

Booking An official warning to a player given by the referee.

Clearance Kicking or heading the ball out of defence.

Cross Sending the ball from the sideline to the centre of the field, usually into the other team's penalty area.

Cushioning Slowing the ball down to control it by using a part of your body.

Dribbling Moving the ball under close control with a series of taps and nudges.

Foul To break one of the rules of football.

Fourth referee In professional football, as well as the referee's assistants there is often a fourth official to help the referee during the match.

Instep The top of your foot where the laces of your boots are.

Interception When a player gets to an opponent's pass first and steals the ball.

Jockeying The skill of delaying an opponent with the ball.

Lay-off A short pass.

Marking Standing close to and guarding a member of the other team whilst that team attacks.

Penalty kick A free shot at goal taken from the penalty spot.

Referee's assistants Two officials who help the referee to run a match.

Set plays The play that comes directly after a restart, such as a kick off, a free kick, a corner or a throw in.

Shielding Placing your body (without committing a foul) between the ball and an opposition player to protect the ball.

Substitute A player who comes on to the pitch during a match to take the place of another player.

Tackling Using your feet to take the ball away from an opponent.

Websites

www.fifa.com

The official website for the organisation that runs world football, it includes news, features and details of all the World Cups.

www.uefa.com

The website of the Union of European Football Associations, the organisation that runs the European Championship and the Champions League.

www.thefa.com

Home of the English Football Association with news on the national team, clubs and league tables, and the FA Cup.

www.shekicks.net

This website offers in-depth coverage of women's football with links to club and competition websites.

www.footy4kids.co.uk/

A website full of great coaching tips and tactics.

www.clivegifford.co.uk

The website of author Clive Gifford, with a dedicated section on football containing quotes, links and training and playing tips.

Index